Colin Pressdee's

STREETWISE
C O O K E R Y

BBC
CYMRU
WALES

Published by
BBC Cymru Wales,
Broadcasting House,
Llandaff, Cardiff CF4 2YQ

Edited and designed by Surrexit
Typeset in 10 on 12 Bembo
Cover photography by Richard Bosworth
Recipe photography by Harry Williams
Printed by Zenith Group, Pontypridd

© BBC Cymru Wales 1992
First published 1992

ISBN 0 9518988 1 7

CONTENTS

PREFACE

Colin Pressdee was brought up in Swansea and from an early age was surrounded by the fruits of the land and the sea. His father was a keen gardener and fisherman in Swansea Bay and Gower.

As a youngster he used to spend months on end at Rhossili on the Gower Peninsula, fishing for all kinds of seafood, including crab and lobster. He also became a keen river fisherman on the Tywi, Cothi and Wye, where he still fishes every season at Builth Wells.

Colin Pressdee has worked as an Export Manager for a seafood marketing company, which took him all over Europe where he learned the delights of regional continental cuisine.

He then became a restaurateur, a partner in the Oyster Perches in Swansea, and proprietor of one of the most renowned restaurants in Wales, the Drangway. Here he specialised in seeking out the very best of local ingredients from the markets to the many small fishing villages throughout west Wales. These ingredients and recipes now form the basis of this book.

He continues to keep an interest in the restaurant business as a marketing consultant to Hilaire's on the Old Brompton Road in London, and is a consultant to the catering, food and drinks industry.

His broadcasting career began in the early 1980s with local radio in Swansea, and since 1988 he has been engaged by the BBC as food presenter for the Radio Wales *Streetlife* programme, BBC Network Television's *Summer Scene*, and BBC Wales's television series *See You Sunday*.

This is Colin Pressdee's first book.

Radio recipes

I n 1988 I was invited by BBC Radio Wales to be the resident food presenter for their daily *Streetlife* programme. This book, based on the quick and tasty recipes we feature in the programme, is a quick guide to make the humblest of chefs 'Streetwise' in the art of good food.

Cooking on radio seems an unusual concept, and indeed it is somewhat like being a radio ventriloquist. Every Monday and Thursday, the *Streetlife* studio at Broadcasting House in Cardiff is miraculously transformed into a mini camp-type kitchen. Apart from the fire extinguisher, the only equipment at hand is an electric frying pan, although we sometimes also use a food processor and a microwave oven.

It goes to show that many of the recipes in the programme and this book can be prepared simply and quickly, using readily available and usually inexpensive ingredients, allowing you at home to prepare tasty meals in about ten minutes with minimum effort and very little mess.

Although we may only cook a small amount in the studio for one or two people, all the Streewise recipes can be adapted to suit a family. Sometimes we may use some unusual luxury ingredients – such as grouse – but the recipes will always adapt to ingredients that are available from your local store. I feel that if you have to eat to live, you may as well eat interesting and tasty food.

Variety is the spice of life for the true enjoyment of food. Even the greatest dishes become tiresome if you have them too often. The seasons provide the variety, and I still prefer to follow our local seasons for fresh produce – even though most produce is available all year round these days.

This book aims to help you recognise the ingredients you need when shopping, rather than spending ages searching for ideas in a supermarket. It will also introduce you to some specialist products that are so useful in enhancing flavours at very little cost. As long as you have a cooking pot, chopping board, a few chef's knives, and a reasonable area in which to work, the majority of these recipes should be within the grasp of the most modest enthusiastic cook.

The cooking way

C ooking techniques have evolved over the years from using direct heat, indirect heat, cooking in an enclosed chamber, and cooking in liquid – commonly known as grilling, frying, roasting and boiling.

Grilling

This applies to both a traditional overhead grill and heating from below, as in a barbecue. In almost every instance the golden rule is to preheat the grill so that the meat is sealed quickly to retain its juices, and that it is turned to the other side to cook evenly.

The texture of the meat, fish or vegetable, its thickness, and the heat of the grill determines the cooking time. This is best judged by observing the browning process. Don't be tempted to squash the meat or fish during grilling as this will break its texture and lose the meat's liquid, making it unpalatable.

I always believe in seasoning meat after it's sealed, allowing it to rest for a short while after cooking for it to set. My three secret S's of cooking are Seal, Season, Set.

Frying or sautéeing

This involves sealing the meat both sides in a pan with a little oil or fat as a cooking medium. Very often the meat is coated in flour to form a crisp crust with the hot fat, but generally I prefer to leave it plain.

You can fry several different meats and vegetables together so that the flavours mix together. Classic Chinese stir-frying gives you an infinite number of possible combinations of flavours. It's important that the dishes are cooked quickly to retain crispness and flavour.

When you deep fry, the food is totally immersed in very hot fat or oil. Meat and fish is usually coated in a batter to seal the flavours.

Cooking by exchange

Many dishes begin as fried or sautéed, but they're then transformed by adding liquid. This releases into the liquid the flavours sealed within the meat to form a sauce. The flavour from the sauce then enters the meat, making a ragoût.

Many of the Streetwise recipes follow this method of cookery, as the cooking pot, in which many of the recipes featured in the *Streetlife* programme and this book are cooked, lends itself so well to this style.

Roasting & baking

Cooking in an oven involves all-round heat being applied evenly to the food. It's most applicable for large pieces of meat or fish that require a long cooking time due to the actual bulk of the food.

When roasting, we should follow a pattern when cooking meat, remembering the three S's.

The meat should be trimmed, boned, stuffed or tied according to the recipe, and put in a roasting tin that will take the joint easily, but without too much room for the fat and juices to spread and burn.

Always preheat the oven so the meat will seal quickly, but remember that a large joint in a small oven will decrease the temperature and slow this process drastically. An initial blast of heat at maximum temperature is necessary to seal the meat properly.

Oiling the meat will speed the browning process – sealing the outside. Season and baste the meat during the cooking, then put on a server in a warm place to set before carving.

Cooking times will vary according to the size of the joint and particular cut, and to one's own preference on how well cooked the meat should be.

Boiling

This technique is often thought only to apply to vegetables, but there's no other cooking technique that gives you such perfect temperature control. Simmering water is perfect for cooking fish, whether a whole large salmon, or an individual steak from a fish.

Apart from temperature control, water is also a medium for transferring flavours, and it's certainly worth making a court bouillon (as described on page 48 whatever meat, fish or even vegetables are to be cooked.

Food cooked in a simmering bouillon will be sealed quickly to retain its flavour. As the cooking process proceeds the transfer of flavours of a court bouillon slowly takes place, not only giving a wonderful flavour to the meat or fish, but also making a stock containing all the goodness possible. This can form a sauce or soup, or can be an integral part of the dish.

Boiled meats or fish are delicious cold as well, and can be left to cool completely in the liquid. This lets the meat absorb more of the flavours from the stock, giving you an exquisite, succulent result.

The same rules apply to poaching small pieces of meat, fish or vegetables. The cooking time can be very short, compared to grilling or roasting, and it's a far more efficient way of using energy.

A corollary of poaching is steaming. This uses steam – evaporated boiling water – to cook, and is very efficient in retaining flavour within the ingredient, and hence some seasoning may need to be added. Nevertheless, if you use herbs and aromates carefully, they can be transmitted through the steam to flavour the meat.

Chop, pan & pantry

Thousands of kitchen cupboards are jammed with wonderful cooking implements – most of them merely collecting dust. You can do so much with a few appropriate knives, a chopping board, a few spoons, a salt and pepper mill, along with a couple of pans – ideally a covered frying pan, a medium sauteuse pan, plus a medium covered pan for vegetables. I would also choose a food processor – ideally one with a liquidiser attachment.

The standard items you need for almost every meal are generally the dry goods, beginning with salt and pepper. Sugar and vinegar are probably the next in importance, and then all other flavours are secondary but may well be important in the individual dishes.

The cooking medium – fat, oil, water, butter – is not always essential to the flavour of the dish, as these are embodied within them. Many meats, fish and even vegetables can be cooked plainly.

Aromates form the essential background flavours. It's only a few dishes that don't benefit from some extra flavour from onions, shallots, garlic and so on. Many vegetables, particularly celery and carrots add extra depth of flavour to meats, fish and other vegetables.

Useful extras include mustard, tomato purée, herbs, sauces, stocks, olive oil, green and black olives, sun-dried tomatoes, pesto sauce, fresh parmesan cheese, capers, horseradish, anchovies and gherkins.

The only other main items you need are the main ingredients – the meat, fish and vegetables. Happy cooking!

STARTERS

mushroom salad

savoury leek & cheese pancakes

salade au fromage blanc

welsh rarebit

guacamole stuffed tomatoes

artichoke hearts with pasta

piedmontese peppers

welsh cawl mamgu

cawl bara lawr

leeks à la grecque

gazpacho

melon with carmarthenshire ham
ginger & liqueur

rich consommé julienne

salade paysanne

ham croûtes

MUSHROOM SALAD

INGREDIENTS
1 iceberg lettuce

12oz/350g of medium sized
button mushrooms

2 tablespoons/30ml
of sunflower oil

Seasoning

VINAIGRETTE
¼ pint/150ml
of sunflower oil

1 tablespoon/15ml
of walnut oil or olive oil

½ tablespoon/7.5ml
of white wine or sherry vinegar

1 shallot, finely chopped

1 clove of garlic, crushed

1 large sprig of parsley
finely chopped

1 heaped teaspoon/10ml
of Dijon mustard

Salt and freshly ground
black pepper

The key to a good salad is a tasty vinaigrette. It actually isn't really about vinegar, more about oil. The salad dressing can be 100 per cent oil if it has the right flavour for the accompanying dish. The finest virgin olive oil is often all that is required, and to drown this with vinegar would destroy the exquisite flavour of the oil.

For this mushroom salad we use a raunchy flavoured garlic and mustard vinaigrette, that will make this a simple and quick cold mushrooms with garlic.

This dish is appetising cold, but heated quickly in a pan or microwave it is equally scrumptious!

METHOD
Thinly slice the mushrooms and sauté very quickly in the sunflower oil for about 30 seconds just to seal. Season with salt and pepper. Tip into a bowl.

Combine the ingredients for the vinaigrette in a jar, screw on the lid and shake until all the ingredients mix well. Test for seasoning and pungency, adjusting as necessary.

Pour the vinaigrette spoon by spoon over the mushrooms, mixing well to coat with the vinaigrette.

Thinly slice the iceberg lettuce and place on a plate and top with the mushrooms. This may be served warm or cold, and will keep in the refrigerator for several days.

Serves 6 as a starter.

SAVOURY LEEK & CHEESE PANCAKES

INGREDIENTS

PANCAKES

1 egg

2oz / 50g of plain flour

1/4 pint / 150ml of milk

Pinch of salt

1 dessert spoon / 10ml
of sunflower oil

FILLING

1lb / 450g of leeks

8oz / 225g of curd cheese
(low fat soft cream cheese)

1/2 a pint / 275ml
of tomato juice

1 heaped teaspoon / 10ml
of pesto sauce

Seasoning

2oz / 50g of grated cheese
(optional)

A delicious hot leek dish – ideal for lunch or as a starter. Leeks cook very well in the microwave. Add a tiny amount of water, oil and seasoning, cover with cling film, and microwave for about a minute.

METHOD

Mix the pancake ingredients together in a bowl, until its consistency is that of runny cream. Cover and leave in a cool place for at least an hour for the ingredients to develop.

In an 8"/20cm pan lightly oiled over a medium heat, pour one dessert spoon/10ml of the pancake mix. Tilt to allow this to completely cover the bottom of the pan. Cook for about a minute until lightly browned underneath. Using a spatula turn the pancake and cook for some 30 seconds on the other side. Prepare 8 pancakes.

To keep the pancakes, place a small piece of butter paper or grease-proof paper between each pancake, so that they can be easily separated. These can be prepared in advance.

Wash the leeks (see page 22) and cut into small 1/4"/5mm dice, and sauté in a little butter until quite soft. Season with salt and freshly ground pepper, and some pesto if desired.

Mix with the curd cheese into a smooth paste. Place one tablespoon/15ml of the mix at the centre of each pancake, then spread out to the edges. Roll up the pancakes.

Mix the pesto in the tomato juice then heat in a pan. Place the stuffed pancakes into this sauce, cover and heat for about 4-5 minutes. Serve hot.

SALADE AU FROMAGE BLANC

INGREDIENTS

1 iceberg lettuce

1 endive

1 radiccio — or a combination of lettuce you like

2 tomatoes

¼ cucumber

2 sticks of celery

4 spring onions

¼ pint/150ml of vinaigrette see page 10

½lb/225g of fromage blanc

20 half-inch square/1cm² croûtons

Happily we can now buy fromage blanc in all supermarkets and even corner stores. The best is made from skimmed milk. This heavier curd cheese is fine for this dish, but is most useful in many cold pâtés and mousses, as it gives an impressive lightness.

Instead of fromage blanc, you could use goat's cheese, cottage cheese, or ricotta.

METHOD

Wash, clean and drain the lettuce carefully, and rip or cut into convenient pieces. Slice the tomatoes, cucumber and celery and mix carefully into the lettuce.

Put the fromage blanc into a bowl, add some of the vinaigrette and fork together to mix. It should be marbled, rather than a smooth paste.

Add a few spoons of plain vinaigrette to the salad and mix carefully. Arrange on a plate and then spoon over the fromage blanc mix. Top with some fresh herbs and the croûtons, and serve.

WELSH RAREBIT

INGREDIENTS

4oz/110g of grated
cheddar cheese

4 tablespoons/60ml
of beer or sherry

½ teaspoon/2.5ml
of mustard

Good twist of black pepper

1 egg

4 rounds of hot buttered toast

Welsh rarebit is a good snack or a savoury after a meal. Any hard cheese may be used, but a medium cheddar has sufficient sharpness for most people. Beer gives a good strong taste, whereas sherry makes it richer and sweeter according to the style used.

For a real Welsh flavour try spreading a little laverbread onto each round of toast.

METHOD

Melt a little butter in a pan and add the grated cheese, the beer and mustard. Heat gently until a smooth sauce is formed.

Whisk the egg and stir into the mixture. Stir well away from the heat not allowing the mixture to boil.

Season with some freshly ground pepper and pour over the hot buttered toast and either serve immediately or pop under a hot grill for a few seconds to brown evenly.

VARIATION

For an Irish Rarebit proceed as above but rather than adding the egg, add two finely chopped small gherkins and a dash of Worcestershire sauce or vinegar. Serve without browning.

GUACAMOLE STUFFED TOMATOES

INGREDIENTS

2 medium sized ripe
avocado pears

Juice of 1 lemon, and the
same quantity of olive oil

1 shallot, very finely chopped

1 clove of garlic, crushed

Salt and freshly ground
black pepper

1 small green pepper
very finely chopped (optional)

1 large sprig of fresh parsley
finely chopped

Other fresh herbs as available

A good dash of tabasco sauce

6 large fairly ripe tomatoes

Avocado pears are most seductive and have a very sensual texture and flavour, until you forget them and they turn from a beautiful pastel green to a khaki brown, when their appeal diminishes. A bowl of brown guacamole looks unappetising

To prevent this you need plenty of lemon juice in the mix. Sprinkle the mix with more lemon juice and seal completely with cling film.

In the refrigerator it will then keep its colour for hours, even days.

METHOD

To skin the tomatoes plunge into boiling water for a few seconds – the skins will remove easily – or leave the skins on.

Halve the tomatoes and scoop out and discard the seeds. Halve the avocado pears and scoop out all the pulp into a bowl.

Mash well with a wooden spoon then add the other ingredients, herbs etc, mixing well. Season and test for pungency. This may be done in the food processor.

Cover this mixture tightly with cling film and chill until ready to use. It may begin to discolour on the edges which can be carefully removed prior to serving.

To serve, fill each half tomato with the guacamole mix and sprinkle with some finely chopped herbs and serve immediately. The serving platter can be garnished with some finely shredded iceberg lettuce which gives a good colour contrast.

ARTICHOKE HEARTS WITH PASTA

INGREDIENTS

1 x 16oz/660g tin
of artichoke hearts

1 onion, finely diced

1 tablespoon/15ml of olive oil

1 red pepper in ½"/1cm pieces

1 teaspoon/5ml of tapenade
(black olive purée)

4oz/110g of pasta shells
(or any shape pasta you like)
cooked, drained and tossed in
olive oil

Herbs

Seasoning

The artichoke is a wonderful summer vegetable so popular on the continent.

The Breton artichokes are the largest. When cooked the 'choke' – the centre flowering part is removed to reveal the base or 'fond', which is not unlike avocado in flavour, but solid in texture.

You can buy small cooked artichokes in jars or cans. The entire plant is edible and very useful in salads or with pasta. Also available are 'fonds' in jars and cans. All keep their flavour very well in the preserving process and are reasonably priced.

METHOD

Sauté the shallots until just transparent. Add the peppers and artichoke hearts (cut into fours). Cover and heat through.

Season and add some herbs of your choice – oregano, marjoram etc. Add the pasta shells and tapenade. Stir until all is heated through. The pasta should not be overcooked.

PIEDMONTESE PEPPERS

INGREDIENTS

4 large red peppers

8 fresh plum tomatoes
(if not available use
3 beef tomatoes)

2 fat cloves of garlic

2 teaspoons/5ml
of piri piri (optional)

2 teaspoons/10ml
of pesto sauce
(optional)

2 tablespoons/30ml
of best olive oil

1 small tin anchovy fillets

⅓ pint/75ml of chicken
or vegetable stock

Seasoning

This wonderful dish was introduced to Wales by Franco Taruschio of the famous Walnut Tree restaurant near Abergavenny.

I like to vary the filling, sometimes zipping up the flavour with some piri piri, or making it more pungent with various herbs – particularly basil.

They are equally delicious hot or cold, but have to retain their shape to contain the flavours. Serve as a starter or a garnish for any meat or fish. Thank you Franco!

METHOD

Cut the peppers into two lengthways, removing the pips so each forms a boat to hold the other ingredients.

Place skin-down in a lightly oiled baking dish. Peel and thinly slice the garlic and put into cup of the peppers together with the piri piri and/or pesto if desired.

Skin and de-seed the tomatoes (plunge them into boiling water for 30 seconds, and the skins will split and remove easily). Place one into each pepper. If you use beef tomatoes, place the dome upwards (a ¼ beef tomato is sufficient). Season with salt and freshly milled pepper.

Place one halved anchovy fillet in a criss cross onto each; dribble the olive oil and anchovy juice over. Heat the stock and pour around – not into – the peppers. Cover the tray with foil.

Cook in a moderate oven (mark 6/375°F/190°C) for about 20 minutes until the peppers are just soft and not collapsed.

Serve as a starter, or as a good main vegetarian course omitting the anchovy if desired.

OPPOSITE
PIEDMONTESE PEPPERS
all the flavour is packed into
the cup shape of the peppers
& concentrated during cooking

16

WELSH CAWL MAMGU

INGREDIENTS

*2lb/900g neck of lamb
chopped through the bone to
2"/5cm pieces*

2 tablespoons/30ml of oil

½lb/225g of carrots

½lb/225g of turnips

½lb/225g of swede

1lb/450g of onions

1lb/450g of leeks

Seasoning

3 pints/2 litres of water

1 sprig of thyme

1 bunch of parsley

4 bay leaves

C awl is the traditional Welsh broth made from meat, root vegetables and leeks. The meat used varies according to taste and availability. Many areas had their own cawl speciality using a particular meat or ham and herbs.

This old traditional version is grannie's broth made from neck of lamb.

METHOD

In a large pan sauté the lamb in the oil until nicely brown. Remove and season with salt and pepper.

Cut the vegetables except the leeks into ½"/1cm dice. Sauté in the lamb fat until they turn gold on the edges. Return the lamb and the herbs (parsley stalks only) and cook for 4–5 minutes covered.

Add 3 pints/2 litres of water, bring to the boil and simmer for 2 hours until the lamb is just coming off the bone. Chop the whites of the leeks, add and cook for a few minutes longer.

Remove from the heat and allow to cool completely in a cold place, so the fat will harden on the surface and can be easily removed.

Reheat the cawl and add the green of the leeks very thinly sliced. Chop the remainder of the parsley and add. Check for seasoning and serve.

CAWL BARA LAWR

INGREDIENTS

2 pints / 1 litre of well-cooked
cawl left overnight and de-fatted

1 or 2 leeks

1 or 2 carrots

4oz / 110g of laverbread

1oz / 25g of freshly grated
cheddar cheese (optional)

Some home-made croûtons

1 large sprig of parsley

Seasoning

The two most traditional Welsh dishes are brought together. It may sound odd, but a small amount of laver really gives a great depth of flavour to a good lamb broth.

Naturally the bacon-based cawl is particularly good with some laver. Ideally, if you pick the laver yourself, chop it rather than mince it, so that the leaves mingle in the soup with the other vegetables.

When reheating cawl after removing the fat, some extra carrots and leeks bring back the lovely green and orange colour.

METHOD

Heat the cawl then add the carrots which have been finely sliced. Cook for 1–2 minutes. Cut the leeks into 2"/5cm thin strips and add together with the spoon of laverbread. Cover and cook for 2–3 minutes adding a little more liquid if necessary. Check for seasoning.

Chop the parsley (not too finely) and add half to the cawl. Fill four bowls with the cawl and top with some croûtons and the freshly grated cheddar and the remaining parsley. Serve immediately, piping hot.

OVER
CAWL BARA LAWR
laverbread adds an extra depth
of flavour to this traditional
Welsh broth

LEEKS À LA GRECQUE

INGREDIENTS
4 nice leeks
weighing about 2lb/900g

¼ pint/150ml of vinaigrette
see page 10

2 additional cloves of garlic

1 teaspoon/5ml of olive oil

O ur celebrated Welsh emblem has been taken to the pinnacle of the culinary world by Pierre Koffman whose *terrine de poireaux au vinaigre de cassis* just shows what a great chef can do with a basically simple ingredient.

I first sampled this very simple dish in the Brasserie d'Alsace on the Île St Vincent in Paris.

METHOD

To prepare the leeks trim off any damaged outer leaves and split lengthwise in two cuts starting 1"/2.5cm from the base of the leek, at an angle of 90 degrees to quarter the leeks.

Plunge into a bowl of cold water for a few seconds and shake to remove any trapped earth and grit. Check in-between each layer that the grit has been removed. Split again lengthwise into eight fronds, then cut into 2"/5cm pieces.

In a large covered pan heat about ¼"/5mm of water to which you have added a little salt and a teaspoon/5ml of olive oil. Bring to the boil, add the leeks and cover and cook for about a minute until just tender. Remove and cool the leeks on a cold plate.

Take the vinaigrette mix and add the extra cloves of garlic which you crush immediately prior to adding. Spoon this mix over the leeks, stir carefully and chill.

This will keep in the refrigerator for several days. You may then serve it slightly re-heated in the microwave, or cold on a bed of mixed lettuce with a little more vinaigrette poured over.

PREVIOUS PAGE
LEEKS À LA GRECQUE
a simple combination that
enhances this traditional
vegetable

GAZPACHO

OVER
GAZPACHO
chilled, refreshing,
flavoursome, summery

INGREDIENTS

3 tablespoons/45ml
of virgin olive oil

½ a large cucumber

2lbs/900g of fairly
ripe tomatoes

1 green pepper

1 red pepper

1 small onion

Small bread croûtons

Fresh herbs

Seasoning

This light version of the traditional Mediterranean favourite relies purely on the fruits and vegetables for its texture and flavour. It takes seconds to make, and if the ingredients are kept in the refrigerator, it can be served immediately.

METHOD

Roughly dice the cucumber, tomatoes, peppers and onion, retaining a small quantity of each to be finely diced and serve in separate bowls for the garnish.

Liquidise the vegetables together, not worrying about the pips and skin, then sieve the entire mix to remove all the pips and skin. You may keep a few ripe tomatoes and red peppers to liquidise separately to make a swirling effect in the soup as shown on the next page.

Season with salt and pepper and add virgin olive oil, mixing in well. Refrigerate for at least an hour if the ingredients are not from the cold box.

To serve, whisk the soup thoroughly and check for seasoning and finely chop fresh herbs – tarragon, parsley, coriander etc, and sprinkle on top.

In separate dishes serve the diced vegetables and the crisply fried croûtons which your guests can take as desired. This recipe will serve 4-6 people, depending on their appetite.

MELON WITH CARMARTHEN HAM GINGER & LIQUEUR

INGREDIENTS
1 fairly ripe melon
(Ogen or Charantais)

12 very thin slices of
Carmarthen or Parma ham

⅓ gill/50ml of liqueur

1 small piece of fresh root ginger
shredded to make about
1 heaped teaspoonful/10ml

Carmarthen ham is sold in the old traditional market in the town of Carmarthen. In the past every farmhouse cured its own hams and bacon, exactly the same way as the other European farming communities.

The hams vary in style according to the length of time in the curing process. The legs – or gammons – make the finest ham, and when aged for several months they can be sliced thinly and eaten as Parma or Bayonne ham. Carmarthen ham is one of the great Welsh delicacies that can form part or the centre of a Welsh feast.

METHOD

Mix together the ginger and the liqueur (such as Cân-y-delyn Welsh whisky liqueur, or Glayva Scotch whisky liqueur).

Quarter the melon, removing the seeds, and adding any excess juice strained into the Cân-y-delyn. Slice off the skin in nice shapes and arrange on a plate.

Spoon over the Cân-y-delyn and ginger mixture, then top or surround with the thinly sliced Carmarthen ham. Delicious!

PREVIOUS PAGE
MELON WITH CARMARTHEN
HAM GINGER & LIQUEUR
light traditional melon and
ginger contrasts with the deep
mature flavour of the ham

Rich Consommé Julienne

INGREDIENTS

*2oz/50g of carrot
cut into juliennes
(large matchstick-size pieces)*

*2oz/50g of white turnip
cut into juliennes*

*2 plump shallots
cut into thin strips*

*4 solid white
button mushrooms
cut into juliennes*

*8oz/225g of chicken breast,
cut into thin strips*

Seasoning

¼ pint/150ml of water

*1 glass/125ml of white
wine (optional)*

*1 glass/125ml of port
(optional)*

*1 1lb/450g tin of good
quality consommé*

*1 small leek
cut into fine juliennes*

Parsley for garnishing

A well made consommé is a great dish. It is also very time consuming. However quality canned versions are good, as the flavour develops from very long cooking, and the canning process actually helps this. Judicious additions to a consommé can make it more interesting and variable.

METHOD

Sauté the carrots and turnips in a little oil for about a minute until just beginning to soften. Then add the shallots and the mushrooms and cook for a further 30 seconds. Add the chicken pieces, stir-frying well until they just firm up. Season and add the wine and water and bring just to the boil.

Add the tin of consommé, bring to a simmer. Then add the julienne of leeks and the port. Serve very hot, garnished with freshly chopped parsley.

SALADE PAYSANNE

INGREDIENTS

1 large bowl of mixed green
lettuces, washed and dried
carefully. A 12"/30cm bowl,
4"/10cm deep is a good size

4oz/110g of smoked streaky fat
bacon, cut in ½"/1cm pieces

8oz/225g of cooked
new potatoes, cold, cut into
¾"/2cm chunks

2oz/50g of shallots
thinly sliced

4 slices of French bread
½"/1cm thick

1 small clove of garlic, crushed

¼ pint/150ml of good
olive oil, extra virgin

1 tablespoon/15ml
of white wine vinegar

1 small bunch of fresh
tarragon or basil

Seasoning

OPPOSITE
SALADE PAYSANNE
a hearty rustic salad makes a
marvellous lunch in the summer

There can be many versions of this French country dish according to the region. This one is based on my first experience at Le Petit Truc at Vignolles near Beaune in Burgundy. Like so many great little country restaurants this is no longer there; but the memory of Édith's salade – and her many other dishes – will not fade.

METHOD

Sauté the bacon in a little oil until crispy. Remove and keep just warm. Sauté the bread in this oil until light golden. Spread the garlic onto the bread. Remove and keep warm with the bacon.

Sauté the shallots in this juice, adding a little more oil if necessary, until just soft. Add the potatoes and fry quickly until going crisp on the edges, adding some of the herbs and a little seasoning. Remove and keep warm.

De-glaze the pan with the vinegar, reducing to about half, adding some more herbs. Add the remaining oil and mix quickly to a light emulsion, but only just warming. Pour some over the salad and mix well. Dress the top of the salad with the potatoes, bacon and halved croûtons. Pour over the rest of the oil, dress with more herbs and serve. The cold lettuce and hot ingredients go together very well.

You can add other cold, blanched green vegetables to the salad leaves, and some other vegetables to the potatoes. The vinegar reduction may contain some Dijon mustard and other herbs and spices according to taste, and the other dishes you are eating.

HAM CROÛTES

INGREDIENTS
4oz / 110g of ham trimmings
finely chopped

2 tablespoons / 30ml of cream

2 egg yolks

1 shallot, finely chopped

1 bunch of parsley
finely chopped

4 rounds of crispy fried
brown bread (in walnut oil)

I f you have a piece of cooked ham, there are always plenty of trimmings from the hock or edge which can be used in a variety of ways for a quick tasty snack.

METHOD

Fry the finely chopped shallot in the butter until soft then add the ham and stir for a few minutes until it is hot. Whisk the egg yolks and the cream together, and add to the pan, stirring carefully, until the mix thickens and add a little of the parsley.

Meanwhile prepare the fried bread cooked with a little walnut oil. Spoon the mix evenly onto the bread. Either serve topped generously with parsley, or place under a hot grill and lightly brown before serving.

SEAFOOD

SHELLFISH

oysters sautéed with shallot vinegar

gratin of cockles with laverbread

angels on horseback

cockles dijonnais

mussels provençale

mussels and rice salad

scallops au gratin

crab with couscous and mayonnaise

crab gumbo

FISH

monkfish in seaweed sauce

cod with ginger & spring onion

salmon mayonnaise

bouillabaisse galloise

red mullet in its own sauce

OYSTERS SAUTÉED WITH SHALLOT VINEGAR

INGREDIENTS

4-6 oysters per person

4oz/110g of small leeks
whites only, sliced into
very thin rings

4oz/110g of unsalted butter

4 small shallots
very finely diced

2 tablespoons/30ml
of good white wine vinegar

Parsley to garish

"The oyster has been eaten and appreciated in almost every country where civilisation has spread, since the days when eating ceased to be a mere necessity and became an art" (H Bolitho in *The Glorious Oyster*).

Oysters have to be fresh and very much alive when opened and eaten immediately. I have only once been ill after oysters, not because of the shellfish but because of the full bottle of brandy I also enjoyed with them. Be warned!

METHOD

Remove the oysters and all juice from their shells retaining the deep shells for serving. Wash the shells to remove any residual mud, particularly around the hinges.

Sauté the leeks in half the butter in a covered pan with a little oyster juice to provide seasoning (you can heat the oyster shells in the same pan or in a warm oven).

Place the warm oyster shells on serving plates and fill each with the sautéed leeks. Keep warm.

In the remaining juice, sauté the oysters rapidly for a second so they just begin to firm. Place one into each shell, add the shallots to remaining juice, heat rapidly, add the wine vinegar and reduce slightly, then whisk in a few knobs of unsalted butter.

Spoon mix over each oyster and serve immediately.

OPPOSITE
OYSTERS SAUTÉED
WITH SHALLOT VINEGAR
the oysters should only just be
cooked for the texture to firm
up slightly

GRATIN OF COCKLES WITH LAVERBREAD

INGREDIENTS
*8oz/225g of cooked
de-shelled cockles or mussels
or a combination of both*

8oz/225g of laverbread

*2oz/50g of freshly grated
breadcrumbs*

*1oz/25g of freshly grated
cheddar cheese*

Seasoning

OPTIONAL EXTRAS
*2 cloves of garlic
finely chopped*

*Generous amount of parsley
finely chopped*

Spring onions, chopped

The Burry inlet in North Gower has been a traditional estuary fishery for cockles and mussels for centuries

The boiling plants of Penclawdd and Crofty were also used for preparing laverbread – the silky green-black seaweed gathered in the bays of South Gower and Pembrokeshire.

Laverbread was as much a part of south Wales as coal mining in the nineteenth century. Now it is considered a delicacy.

This dish is a celebration of the seafoods of the fishermen of Penclawdd. A unique combination of cockles, mussels and laverbread.

METHOD

Take four shallow gratin dishes and divide the laverbread between them, spreading a thin layer in each dish. Top this with the freshly cooked cockles and/or mussels and a small amount of the liquid, and generously heap the breadcrumbs and the cheddar cheese on top. You may mix the breadcrumbs with the optional extras for extra colour and flavour.

Place in a medium oven (mark 6/375°F/ 190°C) or under a grill for about 5 minutes until the whole dish is sizzling and golden brown. Serve immediately.

Serves 4.

*OPPOSITE
GRATIN OF COCKLES
WITH LAVERBREAD
Penclawdd on a plate;
the one I showed Keith Floyd*

ANGELS ON HORSEBACK

INGREDIENTS

12 oysters de-shelled

2oz/50g of shallots or spring onions, finely sliced

12 very thin rashers of smoked streaky bacon weighing 6oz/175g

12 cocktail sticks

4 thin slices of brown bread

1 teaspoon/5ml of vegetable oil

1 tablespoon/15ml of walnut oil

This is one of the great savouries – also delicious as a hot canapé. 'Devils' are prunes cooked in bacon.

You may substitute the oysters in this recipe with chicken, goose, duck liver (cut into 12 small pieces) if your guests do not like oysters.

You can use fresh oysters or the frozen oyster meats. Canned or smoked oysters are also very acceptable.

METHOD

If using fresh, frozen oyster or chicken livers seal them in a pan in a little hot oil to just firm for about 5 seconds. Sauté the finely sliced shallots in a little oil until soft and allow to cool.

Take each rasher of bacon, place on oyster with a small amount of shallot and roll up into a roulade and secure each with a cocktail stick. Either fry quickly in a covered frying pan until the bacon is crisp on the outside, or grill under a hot grill.

Using a pastry cutter, make 4 rounds of bread about 3"/7.5cm in diameter. Fry these in the vegetable oil, to which you have added the walnut oil, until slightly brown. Remove and keep warm.

Remove the cocktail sticks from the bacon and place three onto each piece of toast. Any residual oyster juice should be slightly heated and poured over the roulades. Serve with some tabasco or hot red pepper sauce.

COCKLES DIJONNAIS

INGREDIENTS

1lb / 450g of cockles

4oz / 110g of shallots
finely chopped

1 tablespoon / 15ml
of mild Dijon mustard

1 glass / 125ml
of dry white wine

8oz / 225g of ripe tomatoes
peeled, seeded and chopped to
about the size of the cockles

Freshly ground black pepper

Freshly chopped chives

¼ pint / 150ml of double cream
(optional)

2oz / 50g of cheddar cheese
(optional)

A cockle is a small clam that lives in the sand. It is usually sold ready-cooked and de-shelled. Frozen cockles are good, but defrost them naturally and retain any juice. Never soak them to defrost as you will wash away the flavour. This dish is very good using frozen prawns slowly defrosted, never soaked. They will cook very quickly. You can use passata (creamed tomato pulp) but the chunkier tomato flesh is better.

METHOD

Sauté the finely chopped shallots in the olive oil until transparent. Mix together the Dijon mustard and the white wine and add to the shallots. Bring to the boil, stirring well.

Add the cockles and the tomato pulp and stir carefully to mix and coat the cockles well, and simmer for 1-2 minutes. For a more liquid dish add the cream and heat through. Serve in small bowls or scallop shells, or top with a little grated cheese and brown under the grill.

MUSSELS PROVENÇALE

INGREDIENTS

One 4½lb/2kg pack of
fresh mussels (available from
fishmongers)

4 shallots, finely chopped

4 cloves of garlic, crushed

2 tablespoons/30ml
of finely chopped parsley

1 sprig of thyme

1 large sprig of fresh oregano
or ½ teaspoon/2.5ml of dried

2 tablespoons/30ml of
virgin olive oil

1 glass/125ml of good
dry white wine

1lb/450g of large tomatoes
de-skinned and pipped, chopped
to ½"/1cm dice

Freshly milled pepper

Mussels are bi-valve molluscs that are filter feeders. Hence the cleaner and purer the water the better. They are in season in the winter 'R' months – September to April.

If bought fresh they should have tightly closed shells, and look and smell fresh. The occasional gaping or broken shelled mussels should be discarded.

If you collect your own, pick them on a spring tide, as low on the beach or rocks as possible. Always cook mussels in a pan with a tight fitting lid so they steam at a high temperature killing any possible bugs!

METHOD

Wash the mussels in cold water, removing the beard and any remaining barnacles.

Sauté the shallots in the oil until transparent, add the crushed garlic then the wine and herbs, and simmer for 2 minutes. Season with black pepper, but no salt. Add the mussels, cover the pan then raise heat and cook quickly, shaking the pan regularly, until the shells are wide open (3-5 minutes usually).

Using a slotted spoon, remove the mussels and take off one shell, placing them cup shell down on a serving platter. Add the chopped tomato pulp to the juice in the pan and cook quickly for 1-2 minutes. Add more fresh herbs, then check for seasoning and pour over the mussels. Sprinkle generously with freshly chopped parsley and serve very hot.

Serves 4-6.

OPPOSITE
MUSSELS PROVENÇALE
lots of beautiful flavours
& colours working together

MUSSELS AND RICE SALAD

INGREDIENTS
*2lbs/1kg of fresh
mussels in the shell
(or the pasteurised frozen
mussels freshly defrosted
reserving all juice)*

*2oz/50g of plump shallots
finely chopped*

2 tablespoons/30ml of oil

1oz/25g of butter

*1 good sprig of parsley
roughly chopped*

1 good sprig of thyme

3 bay leaves

Black pepper

1 glass/125ml of white wine

*8oz/225g of basmati rice
(well rinsed)*

½ iceberg lettuce, shredded

*2 tablespoons/30ml
of mayonnaise (home made or a
good quality brand), or freshly
chopped herbs*

Mussels can now be bought frozen in 1kg vacuum packs. These are the best alternative to fresh. Ask your fishmonger for them—they come from Myfi Mussels in north Wales.

No part of the mussel is poisonous, but the beard or 'bissus' is indigestible if eaten in very large quantities. Quickly check inside the lips of each mussel after cooking. Remove any obvious bissus before cooking.

METHOD

Sauté the shallots in butter and oil until transparent. Add the wine and the herbs and a good twist of black pepper, and simmer for 4-5 minutes.

Add the mussels, raise the heat, cover the pan and cook for 3 minutes, until all the shells are open and the mussels well cooked (if you are using the pasteurised mussels, you can decrease the cooking time, but remember to add all the defrosted juice into the pan).

When mussels are cooked, drain off the juice into another pan, measuring the quantity, making up the volume of liquid with water or wine to double the volume of the rice.

Bring to the boil and let the rice slowly cook, covered, for about 10-12 minutes. Pour into a bowl to cool. Meanwhile de-shell the mussels. When the rice is cool stir in the mayonnaise. Garnish with mussels and herbs. Serve on a bed of shredded iceberg lettuce.

SCALLOPS AU GRATIN

INGREDIENTS

1lb/450g of scallops
(8-12 depending on size)

2 shallots

2 egg yolks

½lb/225g of unsalted butter

1 tablespoon/15ml
of tarragon vinegar

A little water

2 teaspoons/10ml
of Dijon mustard

2oz/50g of finely grated
cheddar cheese

Seasoning

S callops were inexpensive when landed in quantity in Cardigan Bay. Sadly not so any more. You can make this dish with any white fish, eg cod, or a combination of fish and shellfish. It's very rich but delicious!

METHOD

First make a Hollandaise sauce: heat the vinegar with a little water and a teaspoon of the shallots and reduce very slightly. Whisk in the mustard, which has been thinned with a little white wine. Cut the butter into small pieces so that it will soften, then on a low heat whisk the egg yolks into the vinegar mix until it is light and frothy, but not curdling.

Remove from the heat and whisk in the butter in small pieces so that all has been absorbed and the sauce has the consistency of a mayonnaise.

Meanwhile sauté the remaining shallots in a little butter until transparent. Add the scallops, which have been halved, keeping the roes whole, and cook for just a few seconds until they just begin to shrivel.

Off the heat, add the Hollandaise sauce and stir in well. Then spoon the scallops with the sauce into the scallop shells, which you have heated in hot water. Top each shell with a little finely grated cheese and pop under a very hot grill for about 15–30 seconds maximum, until the cheese is golden. Do not overcook as the scallops will shrivel and the sauce will separate.

CRAB WITH COUSCOUS AND MAYONNAISE

INGREDIENTS
8oz/225g of crab meat
(you may use some of
the dark meat for this)

1oz/25g of butter

4oz/110g of uncooked couscous

Dash of tabasco sauce

½ iceberg lettuce
finely shredded

Fresh herbs and seasoning

A little oil

MAYONNAISE
1 fresh egg

½ pint/275ml of sunflower oil

1 heaped teaspoon/10ml
of Dijon mustard

If available buy a freshly cooked crab – the hen crab you will find has a large quantity of dark meat. This is usually very delicious but quite rich. Remove the meat from the shell, taking care to discard the gills (fingers) and the stomach sack. Crack the claws and remove the white meat.

METHOD

Fork the white and brown meats together, not over-mixing.

To cook the couscous, place it in a bowl and cover with boiling water, stir once then leave it to stand for 5 minutes. Add the butter and microwave for 2-3 minutes, forking every 30 seconds so that the couscous becomes very light and fluffy. Alternatively sauté in the butter in a covered non-stick pan for 2-3 minutes, stirring regularly.

When cold, mix the couscous and the crab meat together, with fresh herbs and 2 tablespoons/30ml of mayonnaise and serve on a bed of shredded iceberg lettuce.

In preparing the mayonnaise, mix the egg and mustard together in a food processor, then while still working, gradually pour in the oil until it thickens. Season with salt and pepper and the juice of half a lemon, working in well.

To make it a little more exotic add a few drops of best quality olive or walnut oil.

To increase the volume of this dish, you can use 8oz/225g of cooked, flaked cod or other suitable white fish.

OPPOSITE
CRAB WITH COUSCOUS
AND MAYONNAISE
the slightly grainy texture &
melty flavour of couscous is
delicious with crab

CRAB GUMBO

INGREDIENTS

*2 tablespoons/30ml
of sunflower oil*

1 onion

1 medium sized green pepper

1 teaspoon/5ml of flour

1 stick of celery

1 clove of garlic

4oz/110g of white crab meat

*½ a fresh white fish (completely
de-skinned and de-boned)*

1 teaspoon/10g of paprika

*bouquet garni of thyme
parsley and orange peel*

*4oz/110g of cooked prawns
(optional)*

1 tin of peeled tomatoes

1 small tin of okra (optional)

¼ pint/150ml of milk

¼ pint/150ml of cream

F resh crabs are landed in quantity in west Wales in the summer. They can be cooked by plunging into boiling, salty water and simmered for 10 minutes. There are no poisonous parts, but the gills or 'fingers' and stomach sack are unpalatable and should be removed. It takes 10-20 minutes to pick the meat from the shell. Hen crabs (recognised by thin, wide tails) have the best dark meat which is rich and very tasty. Cocks have the best white meat from the claws.

Crabmeat can be bought frozen or tinned, but it's expensive. The only way to get cheap crabmeat is to buy the crabs whole and de-shell them yourself. If you use frozen or tinned you can bulk up the meat with some fresh cod or coley.

METHOD

Roughly chop the onion and celery, and sauté for 3-4 minutes. Add the flour, bouquet garni, paprika and cook for 2-3 minutes. Add the garlic, crab meat and the white fish, the tomatoes, okra, plus a little fish stock if available. Heat to boiling point.

Simmer for about 10-15 minutes, then add the milk and cream. Heat through carefully, remove the bouquet garni, add the prawns if desired, and serve.

MONKFISH
IN SEAWEED SAUCE

INGREDIENTS

*1 tail of monkfish, skinned
weighing 1-1½lb/450-700g*

2 plump shallots, finely diced

*2 tablespoons/30ml
of sunflower oil*

Seasoning

2oz/50g of laverbread

2oz/50g of unsalted butter

*½ glass/60ml
of dry white wine*

Chopped parsley for garnishing

Monkfish is the angler fish, known as *rape* in Spain and *lotte* in France. It is the tail of the angler fish and is usually purchased already de-skinned. It has one central bone with small fins but a cross-section looks somewhat like a Barnsley Chop! This recipe is cooking the tail whole and in France this is known as *Gigot de Mer* – just like roasting a leg of lamb. You may cook this dish in a covered pan or in the oven. Allow 4-6oz/110-175g of monkfish per person.

METHOD

Using a covered pan, sauté the tail of monkfish both sides for 2–3 minutes, then add the shallots and stir, spooning over the fish for the flavour to penetrate.

Season with salt and freshly ground black pepper, then cover the pan and allow it to cook for 5-6 minutes until the fish is almost cooked.

Add the dry white wine, cover and continue cooking until the fish is just firm.

Baste the fish with the cooking juices, then remove and keep warm while you finish the sauce.

Add the laverbread to the cooking juices, stir well, add the butter and whisk lightly until a nice smooth, light, creamy sauce is formed.

Slice the monkfish into ¼"-½"/(5-10mm slices off the bone, arrange on a plate, then surround with the seaweed sauce.

Garnish with freshly chopped parsley and serve with some boiled rice.

RED MULLET
IN ITS OWN SAUCE

INGREDIENTS
2lb/900g of red mullet
about 6-8oz/175-225g each

2oz/50g of shallots
finely chopped

3 tablespoons/45ml of olive oil

½oz/10g of butter

1 small glass/125ml of
dry white wine

Dash of cream

Seasoning

Red Mullet is one of my favourite fish. It is caught extensively in the summer and autumn. It is delicious grilled on the bone, leaving the livers inside the fish. They are a bit boney, so if filleted they can be enjoyed without bone problems! The heads and bones make excellent fish stock or soups. Ask your fishmonger to fillet the fish reserving the livers for the sauce. Make sure he de-scales the fish first.

METHOD

Sauté the shallots in the olive oil for under a minute, until transparent. Move to one side of the pan. Add the red mullet fillets, skin side down, cover the pan and cook for about one minute. Do not turn the fish. They should be just firm. Remove and place on a serving platter.

Add the wine to the pan and reduce, stirring in the shallots. Mash the livers into the butter and whisk into the sauce with the pan off the heat. Add a little cream if desired, then pour around the fish, garnishing with some chopped fresh herbs.

One fillet is sufficient as a starter, two or three as a main course.

MEATS

roast nut of lamb with a pesto sauce

sautéed liver in breadcrumbs

stir-fried lamb kidneys

treasures of new season's lamb

mediterranean lamb

best end of lamb with shallots & mushrooms

duck with lentils & turnips

hock of carmarthen ham with chickpeas and tomato sauce

breast of corn-fed chicken with wild mushrooms

chicken dumplings in rich consommé

pork with grain mustard sauce

pork steak with apple & ginger

tenderloin of pork with marjoram

steak with shallot sauce

fillet of beef with oyster sauce

summer oxtail

pigeon with leeks & juniper

ROAST NUT OF LAMB WITH A PESTO SAUCE

INGREDIENTS

*4 chunks of lamb weighing
4-6oz/110-175g each*

4 shallots or 1 onion

4 cloves of garlic

*¼ pint/150ml of good
quality lamb stock*

*½ pint/275ml of fresh tomato
juice or tomato concasse – the
tomato pulp de-seeded,
de-skinned and chopped*

*12 fresh basil leaves or
1 dessert spoon/10ml of
pesto sauce*

S pring lamb to me is the most succulent and flavoursome meat of all. It has a natural fragrance passed from the ewe who spends the summer months on the Welsh hills, developing a dark flesh that takes on an aromatic, slightly gamey flavour.

METHOD

You may use any leanish cut of lamb for this – a piece from the leg, or the noisette – which is the boned and rolled loin. Always remove any excess fat.

Oil the lamb, place in a baking dish and cook in a hot oven until lightly browned and still pink, remove and keep warm.

Pour off any excess fat from the pan and add the shallots or onions with the garlic. Cook until just transparent then add the wine and the lamb stock cooking well until it reduces to half. Add the fresh tomato juice, check for seasoning and chop the fresh basil leaves and add immediately. Cook the sauce for 4–5 minutes until it reduces slightly.

Either serve the sauce on the side with the chunk of meat, or finely slice the meat and garnish with the pesto sauce, which is richly flavoured, highly coloured, and very delicious.

*OPPOSITE
ROAST NUT OF LAMB
WITH A PESTO SAUCE
highly flavoured pesto makes
this rich colourful dish*

SAUTÉED LIVER IN BREADCRUMBS

INGREDIENTS

*8oz/225g of lamb's liver
cut into slices 2" square/5cm²
and ¼"/5mm thick*

1 small bowl of plain flour

1 egg, whisked

*1 bowl of freshly made
breadcrumbs*

*2 teaspoons/10ml of finely
chopped herbs, sage and
tarragon, or half a teaspoon
of dried*

Sunflower oil for frying

L iver is rich in minerals and protein and hence very good for you. However memories of school lunches of leathery liver in thin onion gravy are grim. The finest liver is calf's, but it's expensive. From a new season's lamb it's mild and tender. Pig's liver is stronger, and ox liver the strongest of all. Liver should be lightly cooked or it will go dry and tough. The breadcrumb coating makes it more   attractive for children.

METHOD

Mix the herbs with the breadcrumbs, then dust the liver with the flour, coat lightly in egg, then drench with the herby breadcrumb mixture. Shake off the excess breadcrumbs and fry the pieces of liver either side for about a minute until just crisp.

Serve with some grilled bacon and onions, or just some sautéed potatoes or salad.

This is a very good dish to introduce children to liver and the stronger flavours.

STIR-FRIED LAMB KIDNEYS

INGREDIENTS

6 lambs kidneys
stripped of their suet and
sliced into ¼"/5mm thick by
2"/5cm long strips, discarding
the hard membrane

6 spring onions
trimmed and cut into
2"/5cm pieces

½ a green pepper
cut into ¼"/5mm by
2"/5cm pieces

½ red pepper, cut similarly

2 carrots
cut in ¼"/5mm batons

1 teaspoon/5ml of ginger
cut into ½"/1cm matchstick
pieces

½ glass/60ml of dry sherry

Salt and freshly ground
black pepper

2 tablespoons/30ml
of sunflower oil with
a touch of sesame oil

L amb's kidneys are inexpensive and cook very quickly. The sweetness of the various vegetables in this stir-fry balances the richer, stronger flavour of the kidneys.

METHOD
Prepare all the vegetables, then in a pan over a brisk heat – ideally a wok – stir-fry the vegetables in the sunflower oil, cooking the harder vegetables first, then just cook until crisp.

Remove the vegetables, then add the kidney pieces with sesame oil and stir-fry over a brisk heat until they are just sizzling.

Return all the vegetables, mix together well, season and add the sherry. Serve this, sizzling hot, from the pan with other Chinese vegetables and rice.

TREASURES OF NEW SEASON'S LAMB

INGREDIENTS

4 lamb's kidneys in their suet

4oz/110g of lamb's
sweetbreads
(the thyroid neck breads)

4oz/110g of lamb's liver

8oz/225g of lean lamb

2 shallots

½ pint/275ml of good,
well reduced lamb stock

Freshly chopped basil leaves
(if available)

1 teaspoon/5ml of
baby capers

1 glass/125ml
of dry white wine

Seasoning

OPPOSITE
TREASURES OF
NEW SEASON'S LAMB
these delicacies cooked
individually have contrasting
textures and flavours that come
together beautifully in this dish

Spring lamb has the most succulent offal which is a feast in its own right. The liver is pale and mild; the kidneys are sweet and covered in a creamy white fat; but the prize above all are the sweetbreads (thyroids) from the neck of a young lamb.

METHOD

Take the suet from the kidneys cutting into a ¼"/5mm dice. Trim, slice and quarter the kidneys. Cut the lamb pieces into ½"/1cm cubes, slice the liver into thin 2"/5cm pieces, and trim the sweetbreads.

On a brisk heat, with a little oil, sauté the cubes of suet until golden brown – this will produce the cooking oil for the rest. Sauté the chunks of lamb stirring well until brown on all sides. Remove and keep warm with the suet.

Follow with the kidneys, browning on all sides but not over-cooking. Remove and keep warm, then sauté the sweetbread until just golden brown, then the liver, turning very quickly. Remove and keep all warm.

Add the shallots cooking quickly for 1–2 minutes, pour in the wine and reduce rapidly. Add the lamb stock and allow it to reduce rapidly for 1–2 minutes. Check for seasoning then add the baby capers, by which time the sauce should be getting slightly sticky. Add the butter in small pieces stirring well to absorb into the sauce.

Return the meats to the pan and stir just to coat with the sauce, then arrange nicely on a plate, garnish with some basil or mint leaves and serve with baby boiled new potatoes.

MEDITERRANEAN LAMB

INGREDIENTS

4 lamb steaks
4-6oz/110-175g each

4oz/110g of tomatoes
large and fairly ripe

2 shallots

1 clove of garlic (optional)

4 large basil leaves or
1 teaspoon/5ml of pesto sauce

Salt and pepper

Olive oil

L amb steaks cut from the leg are usually very lean. Cut off any excess fat, leaving a little to brown on the edges. This cut is most tender and cooks in just a few minutes, taking up the pungent flavours of shallots, garlic and basil.

METHOD

Sauté the lamb steaks in a little olive oil until lightly browned on both sides.

De-skin and de-pip the tomatoes, and chop into a ¼"/5cm dice. Finely chop the shallots and garlic and add to the pan – having pushed the lamb steaks to one side.

Sauté for 2-3 minutes then add the tomato and basil (or pesto) and heat through.

Pile this onto the lamb steaks, season, cover pan and cook for 2-3 minutes for the flavours to mix, or longer if you prefer your lamb more well done.

BEST END OF LAMB WITH SHALLOTS & MUSHROOMS

INGREDIENTS

*1 best end of lamb – 6 chops
from below the shoulder blade
in one piece, with the end
(chine) bone removed*

2 shallots finely chopped

12 tiny button mushrooms

*1 small glass / 125ml
of medium dry white wine*

2 sprigs of fresh mint

Seasoning

I like to cook the lamb chops in one piece so the outside can be crispy, and the inside very succulent. If you like lamb more well-done, pop them back into the pan after slicing and cook a few minutes longer.

METHOD

Trim the best end of any surplus fat, just leaving a little close to the meat. Heat a pan with a little oil, and brown the meat on both sides cooking it meat side down (bones uppermost) covered for about five minutes.

Add the shallots, stirring well. Cover and cook for another few minutes. Then add the mushrooms, either left whole or sliced into four and stir.

Season with salt and pepper and cook for a few minutes covered. De-glaze the pan with a little white wine then remove the meat and slice into six chops – the meat should be pink and slightly brown on the edges.

Chop the mint finely and add to the pan, check for seasoning and serve with the lamb chops.

DUCK WITH
LENTILS & TURNIPS

INGREDIENTS

*1 large half duck, weighing
about 2½lb / 1125g on the bone
breast portion*

*8oz / 225g of French brown
lentils*

8oz / 225g of onion, sliced

*4oz / 110g of carrots
cut into strips*

1 stick of celery, in small dice

2 cloves of garlic

*8oz / 225g of white turnips
cut into cubes*

*½ pint / 275ml of a good stock
made from the bones of the duck*

1 glass / 125ml of red wine

*1 tablespoon / 15ml
of red wine vinegar*

Juice of half an orange

*Herbs, a good sprig of fresh
sage and a few bay leaves*

F or this dish you can buy legs of duck in
the supermarket which are inexpensive,
or you can buy a quarter duck where you have
the breast which does have a higher yield of
meat. Each leg will feed one person; each
breast – if a decent size – can feed two persons.

METHOD

Lightly oil the skin of the duck and put on a
tray in a very hot oven for 15 minutes, until
the skin becomes nice and crisp. Remove and
allow to cool, then remove the skin and cut
into small pieces to reserve.

Remove the meat from the bone and cut
into sizeable chunks. Chop and cook the bones,
together with the trimmings of the vegetables,
the peel of the onions and carrot, some celery
and turnips, in about a pint/570ml of water,
until a good stock is formed. Strain off the stock.

Cook the lentils in a little duck fat with a
small quantity of each of the vegetables with
the stock for about 30 minutes, until they are
just soft but not breaking up.

Sauté the rest of the vegetables in a little
duck fat until just soft. Add the pieces of duck
and the red wine and seasoning. Cover and
cook for the wine to reduce to half. By this
time the lentils should be cooked, so add these
plus the juice and a good sprig of sage.

Check for seasoning and add the juice of
half an orange. Simmer for about 10 minutes.

Meanwhile put the pieces of duck skin
back into the oven to crispen up (you can do
this in a small frying pan) and serve the duck
stew in soup bowls, topped with crispy pieces
of duck skin.

PIGEON WITH LEEKS & JUNIPER

INGREDIENTS

2 pigeons, skinned and halved

2 tablespoons/30ml of oil

4oz/110g of bacon cut in 1"/2.5cm pieces

8oz/225g of onion thinly sliced

2oz/50g of carrot cut in rings

12 juniper berries

½ pint/275ml of good stock

8oz/225g of leeks cut into large juliennes

1 large glass/250ml of good red wine

Seasoning

Pigeons have rich, dark, close–fibred meat that should either be cooked quite pink or braised for much longer until it is well done having absorbed the sauce.

METHOD

Sauté the bacon in the oil until just crisp. Remove, then sauté the pigeon pieces in this oil until very lightly browned for 30 seconds either side. Remove, then put in the vegetables, and sauté well until just soft, then return the pigeons to the pan. Add the juniper berries, seasoning and bacon.

Turn the heat up full, and add one large glass of good full-bodied red wine and some of the leeks. Cover the pan and cook over a high heat for 5 minutes. Garnish with more leeks fully sliced, and serve.

In you wish your pigeons to be well cooked, cover and place in a slow oven (mark 3/325°F/170°C) for 30-40 minutes. Then remove the pigeons carefully and mix the juice and vegetables. Add the remaining leek and cook for a further 5 minutes. This will be a nice sauce dish which will have a good pungent flavour, together with the crunch of the leeks. Serve with the pigeon breasts.

BREAST OF CORN-FED CHICKEN WITH WILD MUSHROOMS

INGREDIENTS

4 breasts of chicken
ideally corn fed, or even the
Poulet de Bresse. You could
also use one chicken quartered
and serve a chicken quarter per
person

3½oz/100g of plump shallots

4oz/110g of assorted wild
mushrooms. The best are
Morels, Charentelles, Céps, and
Trompets (which can be bought
from specialist shops). Otherwise
you can use ordinary mushrooms

½ pint/275ml of very good,
well reduced chicken stock

¼ pint/150ml of fresh cream

Fresh herbs
tarragon, basil, coriander

1 glass/125ml of white wine

Corn-fed chicken has more solid flesh with a closer texture and far more flavour than a standard chicken. Wild mushrooms are plentiful in late summer and the autumn.

METHOD

Sauté the chicken in oil, both sides for 2-3 minutes. Add the shallots and cook until transparent. Season well and baste the chicken with the juices.

Cover the pan and cook for 5-10 minutes according to the thickness of the flesh – the legs of chicken will take longer. When just cooked, remove the chicken pieces and keep warm.

Add the cleaned mushrooms. Raise the heat and sauté these well, until just browning lightly on the edges. Add a little white wine and the chicken stock to moisten and cook for 2-3 minutes to allow slight reduction.

Add the cream and heat through, then add the fresh herbs and check for seasoning.

Serve with the chicken pieces. You can either serve the breasts of chicken whole or slice them nicely in a fan arrangement. Always serve the sauce on the plate with the chicken meat on top.

If you pick your own wild mushrooms always identify the species carefully first – there are a few very poisonous ones.

When cleaning wild mushrooms literally dunk them in water and wipe clean. It's worth just cooking them immediately as described and store covered, in the refrigerator.

Chicken Dumplings in Rich Consommé

INGREDIENTS

1 carrot, cut into rings

1 mushroom, cut into thin slices

1 shallot, cut into rings

1 small leek, cut into rings

8oz/225g of chicken breast

2oz/50g of chicken livers

4oz/110g of low fat cream cheese

2 egg whites

1oz/25g of flour

¼ pint/150ml of fresh cream

1 can of good quality consommé

1 small measure/25ml of sherry

1 small piece of ginger sliced very thinly

Seasoning

A colourful way to liven up a consommé to make a light dish with two different dumplings

METHOD

Dice the chicken trimming off pieces of sinew, either pound or place in the food processor and chop finely for about 30 seconds. Add the egg white and beat into a fine paste for about another 30 seconds. Mix in the flour and season with a little white pepper and salt.

Add the low fat cream cheese and mix until smooth. Remove half, and beat into this half the cream and some freshly chopped or dried tarragon, or other fresh herbs.

To the other half of the mixture add the livers and mix well, chopping finely, then add the other half of cream and mix in carefully. Store the mixtures in the fridge until required.

Sauté the carrots and an equal quantity of white turnip in a little oil, until just beginning to soften. Add the shallots and mushrooms and cook for about 30 seconds until just soft.

Season and add a little water, then the consommé, and bring just to a simmer.

Using two dessert spoons, form the dumplings into oval shapes and drop into the soup, putting two of each colour per person. Allow the soup to simmer very quietly until the quenelles are just firm. Add the thinly sliced ginger (optional) and a glass of sherry or Madeira, and serve very hot, garnished with tarragon or parsley.

PORK WITH GRAIN MUSTARD SAUCE

INGREDIENTS

1lb/450g of tenderloins of pork

4 shallots

*1 tablespoon/15ml of oil
(ideally walnut)*

*2 tablespoons/30ml of
coarse grain mustard*

¼ pint/150ml of good stock

*½ glass/60ml of
dry white wine*

¼ pint/150ml of fresh cream

Pork is inexpensive and the tenderloins are quick to prepare and cook. They are a bi-product of the bacon industry and are widely available.

The coarse grain mustard gives a good rustic touch to this dish.

METHOD

Trim the pork and cut into ½"/1cm slices at an angle to obtain largest escallops possible. Flatten to ¼"/5mm.

Sauté the finely chopped shallots in the oil, but do not brown. Push to the side of the pan and sauté the pork quickly to seal and lightly brown on both sides. Season well and de-glaze with wine.

Mix the mustard with the stock and add to the pan, cooking rapidly to reduce to a half. Add the cream, shaking pan to mix well, and heat through. Check for seasoning and serve.

PORK STEAK WITH APPLE & GINGER

INGREDIENTS

4 pork steaks
from the leg, 6oz/175g each

2 shallots

1 Granny Smith apple

1 teaspoon/5ml of fresh ginger
cut into tiny batons

1 tablespoon/15ml
of sunflower oil

½ glass/60ml
of sweet white wine

¼ pint/150ml of good
chicken stock

2oz/50g of unsalted butter

Seasoning

Apple sauce is very traditional with pork. The sweetness of the meat is enhanced by the acidic nuances from the apple. The ginger gives extra depth of flavour.

METHOD

Sauté the steaks in oil for 2–3 minutes each side until lightly browned, season with salt and pepper. Move to the side of the pan then add the shallots and cook until transparent.

Add the ginger and apple, cut into wedges, leaving the skin on. Add the white wine and stock, cover the pan and cook for 5–6 minutes or until the pork is cooked – firm to the touch – basting with the juice occasionally.

Remove the steaks and apple wedges. Arrange on a serving platter and keep warm.

Reduce the sauce slightly, and remove from the heat. Whisk in the butter in small pieces until all is absorbed. Check for seasoning and pour over the steaks.

TENDERLOIN OF PORK WITH MARJORAM

INGREDIENTS

*6oz/175g of tenderloins
of pork, well trimmed*

*4 sprigs of fresh marjoram or
1 heaped teaspoon/10ml of
dried marjoram*

*Salt and freshly ground
black pepper*

2 tablespoons/30ml of olive oil

2oz/50g of butter

Marjoram is a perennial herb that grows easily. It is similar to oregano but less pungent. It can be used freely as it will not overpower the flavours of the meat.

METHOD

Cut the tenderloins diagonally across the grain to form as large an escallop as possible about ½"/1cm thick. Flatten each with a heavy knife or a light steak mallet to about ¼"/5mm thick.

Season with salt and pepper and sprinkle with the fresh or dried marjoram. If you are using dried, go sparingly as this is far more pungent.

Heat the olive oil and the butter until just beginning to turn nutty brown, then fry the escallops for about one minute on either side until lightly golden on the edges. Serve with wedges of fresh lemon, some sautéed or boiled potatoes, and fresh spinach or mange-touts.

Serves 2.

STEAK WITH SHALLOT SAUCE

INGREDIENTS

4 rump steaks
6-8oz / 175-225g each

4 large shallots

2 tablespoons / 30ml
of sunflower oil

1 glass / 125ml
of fruity red wine

¼ pint / 150ml of well-reduced
chicken or veal stock

2oz / 50g of unsalted butter

Seasoning

The best beef is hung in a cold room for many weeks until it takes on a dark colour. Always look for some creamy white fat on the meat, with specks of fat marbled through the lean. This will keep the steak moist during cooking. Again remember the three S's. Shallots are wonderful with good beef

METHOD

Sauté the steaks in a very hot pan until cooked to your liking. Cook the steaks on one side for 2–3 minutes until lightly browned; turn once only and cook for another 2–3 minutes. For a rare steak the meat should still be fairly soft to the touch. When beads of red juice appear on the meat it will be medium–rare. As the beads become larger it is medium. Continue cooking if you prefer it well done.

Season the steaks with freshly ground black pepper and keep just warm.

Add the shallots to the pan with a little more oil if necessary and cook until transparent. Add the wine and reduce slightly, then add the stock and cook for about 10 minutes until the sauce is a nice thick consistency.

Remove the pan from the heat and whisk in the butter in small pieces, until the sauce is slightly frothy and all the butter has been absorbed. Check for seasoning and serve the sauce over the steaks.

You may make the sauce in advance but reheat and whisk in the butter just prior to service.

FILLET OF BEEF
WITH OYSTER SAUCE

INGREDIENTS

1lb / 450g of beef

12 fresh oysters
or 1 can of oysters

1 shallot

1 lemon

2 egg yolks

½ pint / 275ml of cream

Worcestershire sauce

Seasoning

The mineral succulence of the oyster, combined with the richness of the beef, will perk up anyone whose energy level is drooping.

In America this recipe is generally known as *surf and turf*, and can be made equally well with some delicious beef skirting. The sauce is very rich and was made famous by Madame Prunier in her legendary London restaurant in St James's, and is named *Sauce Prunier* after her.

METHOD

Simply cut the beef into ½"/1cm slices. De-shell the oyster reserving all the juice. Finely dice the one shallot. Whisk the yolk of the egg into the cream, mixing well.

In a hot pan quickly sauté the shallot and push to one side of the pan. Then sauté the strips of beef turning once only until cooked to your liking. Season lightly and push to one side of the pan.

Tip the pan slightly, adding the oysters and their juice, and cook quickly for about a minute so they shrivel just slightly. Pour in the egg yolk and cream, mix and stir well with the oysters until the sauce just begins to thicken. Do not boil.

Add a touch of Worcestershire sauce or tabasco. Arrange the pieces of meat on a plate; top each with an oyster; pour the oyster sauce over. Serve immediately.

SUMMER OXTAIL

INGREDIENTS

2 oxtails cut into segments
(ask the butcher to do this)

2 medium onions

1lb / 450g of turnips

2 sticks of celery

2 carrots

4 unpeeled cloves of garlic

8oz / 225g of white grapes

1 pint / 570ml of very dry cider

2 sprigs of thyme

4 bay leaves

12 green peppercorns

Seasoning

1lb / 450g of colourful
vegetables to garnish —
courgettes, carrots, celeriac,
turnips etc all cut into nice
shapes and blanched

Oxtail is a great winter dish which requires long, slow cooking, giving a wonderful deep flavour that warms the dark winter days.

However often in summer I long for this deep flavour, so I devised my summer oxtail stew which has the light colour and lively flavour of summer vegetables combined with an underlying richness.

The key to this dish is to seal the meat without browning, similarly with the vegetables, all of which must be young and light in colour. Long, slow cooking is still the key, and the vegetables puréed to thicken the sauce — definitely no flour!

METHOD

Trim any excess fat from the oxtails. Roughly chop the onions, carrot, celery and turnip and sauté in a little oil for 2 minutes, stirring continually. Add the oxtails, stir and cover, cooking for 5 minutes to seal. Do not allow the vegetables to colour at all.

Stir to mix well. Add all the other ingredients plus some water to just cover. Bring to the boil and simmer gently for about 2 hours. The meat should just be coming from the bone easily, yet still attached. Check for seasoning and remove from the heat and allow to cool.

Using a slotted spoon remove the meat and set aside. Allow the juices to cool so the fat can be separated. Reheat the juices and vegetables. Remove herbs and carrots and liquidise the remainder, sieving to remove the pips etc. Return the meat to the sieved sauce, add the blanched vegetables, heat through thoroughly and serve in large bowls.

HOCK OF CARMARTHEN HAM WITH CHICKPEAS & TOMATO SAUCE

INGREDIENTS

1 hock of ham

8oz/225g of dried chickpeas

1 large carrot, quartered

1 onion, quartered

1 stick of celery, quartered

1 large leaf of fresh lovage

water to cover

8oz/225g of shallots roughly chopped

1lb/450g of ripe tomatoes puréed and sieved

1 glass/125ml of fruity full red wine (eg Shiraz)

A hock of ham has a good amount of meat and lots of flavour. It requires lengthy cooking initially, but then this dish can be put together very quickly.

Any ham may be used if Carmarthen ham is not available.

METHOD

Soak the hock overnight to remove any excessive salt.

Bring to a boil (covered with water), test for saltiness and discard the water if the salt is excessive. Repeat, and when simmering add the vegetables, lovage and chickpeas. Cook briskly for 20 minutes then simmer gently for about 2 hours. Allow to cool.

Remove the meat from the hock in large pieces. Slice some of the skin into strips if you like the skin.

Sauté the shallots in a little oil until soft. Add the meat and wine and heat through quickly. Add the tomato pulp, some chickpeas and some of the stock and vegetables to make up the required amount of liquid. Heat through for about ten minutes and serve in large soup bowls.

Use any excess chickpeas to make a wonderfully flavoured humous!

VEGETARIAN

winter vegetarian rissoles

vegetarian risotto

sautéed field mushrooms with garlic & leeks

laverbread quiche

herb omelette

WINTER VEGETARIAN RISSOLES

INGREDIENTS

1 onion, finely sliced

1 small leek, finely sliced

2oz/50g of mushrooms

8oz/225g of mixed chopped
nuts: walnuts, pecans, peanuts,
brazils, cashews, almonds etc

A little oil for cooking

6 chestnuts. Tinned are fine, or
if using fresh, boil in a little
water until just soft

1 pickled walnut
both chestnuts and walnut just
squashed slightly so they don't
break up too much

Seasoning

Sprig of fresh coriander
(optional)

1 teaspoon/5ml of
purée of coriander

1 teaspoon/5ml of mustard

6 cream crackers
ground into crumbs

1 egg

These vegetarian rissoles are full of winter flavours – nuts, chestnuts and pickled walnuts. They can be made to any shape and can be served as a canapé or a main course.

METHOD

Roughly chop the nuts in the food processor (or bash them with a rolling pin).

Sauté the onion, leeks and mushrooms in a little oil until just soft. Allow to cool then whizz in the food processor for a few seconds.

Add the chopped nuts, and return to the pan and sauté for a few minutes. Add the chestnuts and pickled walnut and mix well.

Tip into a bowl and add the coriander, mustard and the half-crushed crackers. Mix into a pâté. Beat the egg and add. Leave the mixture to cool completely.

Mould the mixture into rissole shapes, coating with the crumbs. These will now store in the refrigerator for several days, or you may freeze them.

To cook, just sauté for 4 minutes on each side. Serve with chutneys, Cumberland sauce etc.

VEGETARIAN RISOTTO

INGREDIENTS

1 onion, cut into rings

1 carrot, cut into batons

1 red pepper, cut into rings

1 green pepper cut into strips

1 clove of garlic, crushed

½lb/225g of mushrooms
as many different varieties as
possible. Bottled and dried are
very good

1 leek, cut into rings

2 tablespoons/30ml of olive oil

8oz/225g of rice

¾ pint/400ml of vegetable
stock; you may bulk it up as
you wish

1 teaspoon/5ml of
mixed or fresh herbs

Freshly grated parmesan cheese

Pinch of cayenne pepper

1 glass/125ml of
medium white wine

A risotto is rice cooked in a stock to absorb the flavours and seasoning contained therein. An interesting combination of vegetables can make a risotto that can be garnished with herbs, nuts or cheese to become quite exotic and very tasty.

METHOD

Sauté the vegetables in olive oil until they are slightly cooked (be generous with the oil). Add the mushrooms later if they are already partially cooked, or if they are the bottled variety.

Add the dried herbs and garlic. Stir in the rice together with a pinch of cayenne pepper. Stir well and cook for 2-3 minutes. Add the glass of medium white wine. Add the liquid, either vegetable stock or water. Stir well, cover the pan and cook for 10 minutes, when most of the water will have been absorbed. Check for seasoning and add some fresh herbs.

Cover and continue to cook for another 3-4 minutes until all the water is absorbed. Top with freshly shaved/grated parmesan cheese and serve.

Sautéed Field Mushrooms with Garlic & Leeks

INGREDIENTS

1lb/450g of field mushrooms

4 cloves of garlic

½lb/225g of leeks

2oz/50g of butter

2 sprigs of parsley

Seasoning

*½ glass/60ml
of dry white wine*

In the late summer and early autumn, particularly in warm, damp weather, field mushrooms grow in profusion. They have a wonderful deep aromatic flavour. You will often see them in local markets, or use the open cup mushrooms that are always available.

METHOD

Clean the mushrooms with a damp cloth. Do not soak them as they absorb water rapidly. Cut into large slices.

Clean and trim the leeks. Cut into fine slices and sauté rapidly in butter for 2-3 minutes. Add the crushed garlic and the mushrooms and stir-fry for a further minute until the mushrooms are just curling. Season and add the wine. Cover and cook rapidly until they are tender. Dredge with finely chopped parsley, and serve in bowls or on toast.

LAVERBREAD QUICHE

INGREDIENTS

*8oz/225g of short crust pastry
rolled thinly to line a
10"/25.5cm quiche mould*

*4oz/110g of finely sliced sautéed
vegetables: onions, carrots, celery
and courgettes, lightly seasoned*

4oz/110g of leeks, sautéed

4oz/110g of low fat cheese

2 eggs

6oz/175g of fresh milk

4oz/110g of laverbread

*1 sprig of tarragon
chopped and dried*

Laverbread adds a very good flavour to many vegetarian dishes. This was always a particularly favourite dish in my wine bars.

METHOD

Line a flan mould with the thinly–rolled pastry.

Sauté the finely sliced vegetables until just soft. Lightly season.

Liquidise, or mix by hand, the milk, eggs and cream cheese. Put in a bowl and add the vegetables, leeks and laverbread and some fresh or dried tarragon.

Pour this into the flan mould. The vegetables will now be evenly distributed throughout the quiche. Top with a little freshly grated cheddar cheese if desired.

Place in an oven (mark 3-4/325°F/170°C) and cook for about 20-30 minutes, depending on oven efficiency, until the quiche is beautifully golden brown on top, and just set.

To serve, either hot straight from the oven, or cold with a salad. It will also heat successfully, if done carefully, in a microwave.

HERB OMELETTE

INGREDIENTS
3 eggs per person
lightly whisked until they
are just beginning to foam

1 small bunch of chives

1 small bunch of parsley

1 small bunch of coriander

2oz/50g of good quality butter

Seasoning

An omelette is a quick meal that can be served plain or with an extensive array of vegetables, herbs and flavourings. The plain omelette cooked in butter is greatly enhanced by a few fresh herbs.

METHOD

Finely chop the herbs (you may use others if desired) immediately prior to making the omelette.

Melt the butter in an 8"-10"/20-25.5cm pan over a medium brisk heat, until just beginning to turn nutty in colour. Pour in the whisked eggs and swirl round the pan to distribute across the bottom of the pan.

Cook over a brisk heat shaking once or twice until beginning to turn gold underneath, evenly distribute the herbs by sprinkling over the top of the omelette and season with a little salt and freshly ground black pepper.

When just beginning to show signs of firmness, roll the omelette onto a plate to form a nice semi-circle with the melted butter poured over. Serve immediately.

DESSERTS

st emilion au chocolat

white chocolate mousse

ice cream & hot chocolate sauce

cappuccino pancakes

summer pudding

gooseberry fool

greengages with fino sherry

pear flan with almonds

elderflower fritters

pears in red wine & cinnamon

macerated peaches in liqueur

kiwi fruit with toasted peanuts

S:T EMILION AU CHOCOLAT

INGREDIENTS

12oz/350g of chocolate

*4oz/110g of crushed
Amaretti biscuits*

1½oz/40g of butter

8 eggs, separated

1 teaspoon/5ml of brandy

Amaretti biscuits are from Italy and are similar to hard macaroons. Their almondy flavour and crunchy texture soak up the brandy.

METHOD

Melt the chocolate. Add the butter, mixing well. Beat in the egg yolks one by one, again mixing well. Whisk the egg whites and fold them into the mixture.

Put some of the Amaretti biscuits and the brandy into the bottom of 3 ramekins. Pour the mixture into the ramekins and chill.

OPPOSITE
ST EMILION AU CHOCOLAT
rich, delicious and decadent!

WHITE CHOCOLATE MOUSSE

INGREDIENTS

12oz/350g of white chocolate

6oz/175g of caster sugar

3 egg yolks

1 whole egg

2 tablespoons/30ml of kirsch

1 pint/570ml of whipping cream

4oz/110g of hazelnuts

1oz/25g of butter

W hite chocolate tends to have a bland over-sweet flavour. This is enlivened by the roasty crunch of the hazelnuts and zip from the kirsch.

METHOD

Melt the chocolate in a bowl over a pan of hot water or in the microwave.

Whisk the sugar, beating well. Add the yolks, one by one, beating well so the mix forms a thick flowing consistency.

Finally beat in the whole egg and add the kirsch.

Whip the cream until stiff, and fold into the chocolate mix. Put into 6 serving bowls and chill in the refrigerator.

Chop or crush the hazelnuts and cook in butter until they are golden brown. Allow to cool, and decorate the mousse with them.

Serves 6.

ICE CREAM & HOT CHOCOLATE SAUCE

INGREDIENTS
*1lb/450g block of ice-cream
directly from the freezer*

HOT CHOCOLATE SAUCE
4oz/110g of plain chocolate

1oz/25g of sugar

*Juice of one orange with
the zest of half an orange*

*4fl oz/100ml of fresh orange
juice or bottled pineapple juice*

¼ pint/150ml of cream

*1 large measure/50ml of
brandy, rum, whisky or gin
(optional)*

Hot chocolate sauce over cold vanilla ice cream is always a hit. You can vary the fruit base – try blackcurrants, morello or black cherries, etc from jars or tins. Strain off the fruit and use the syrup to make the sauce, and add the fruit and juice before serving.

METHOD
De-juice the orange and heat with the sugar, then break the chocolate into small pieces and stir into the hot fruit juice. Add a little sugar to taste and grate in some orange zest using a fine cheese grater. Add the cream and stir in well but do not boil. Then if desired add a large measure of spirit.

Mix well then keep the sauce warm until ready for use. Pour the sauce hot over the ice cream directly from the freezer and serve immediately.

CAPPUCCINO PANCAKES

INGREDIENTS

1 egg

2oz/50g of plain flour

4oz/110g of milk

1 teaspoon/5ml of
powdered chocolate

1 teaspoon/5ml of
powdered coffee

1 teaspoon/5ml of sugar

2 teaspoons/10ml of
melted butter

¼ pint/150ml of
whipped cream

1 measure/25ml of
rum or brandy

Icing sugar

These pancakes have the three sensations of a good cappuccino – the strong flavour of coffee, the airy creamy topping, and the slight sweetness from the chocolate. A touch of spirit adds extra warmth.

METHOD

Mix together the flour, sugar, coffee and chocolate, then mix in the egg and milk to form a smooth pancake batter. Mix in the melted butter and leave to stand for at least 2 hours before making the pancakes.

Use a 6"-8"/15-20cm round frying pan with minimum amount of oil or butter and make the crêpes in the normal way, as thin as possible, placing a small piece of buttered paper between each pancake to stop them sticking.

Whip the cream until firm then sift in a little sugar and a measure of spirit, then put a tablespoon of the cream into the centre of each crêpe and roll up into a roulade. Dust with icing sugar and serve.

OPPOSITE
CAPPUCCINO PANCAKES
triple-barrelled flavour

SUMMER PUDDING

INGREDIENTS

*2lbs/900g of fresh currants,
blackcurrants, redcurrants,
cherries, raspberries, loganberries,
wimberries, blueberries etc*

*1 pint/570ml of a dry
white wine*

*3 tablespoons/45ml
of crème de cassis*

4oz/110g of sugar

*A large sprig of fresh basil
or 4 cloves*

*2 teaspoons/10g of powdered
gelatine*

*10 thin slices of de-crusted
white bread*

This wonderful dish made from summer fruits has the fragrance of a hedgerow on a summer evening, and the depth of flavour only produced by non-ripened fruit,

When berries become scarce you can use dried fruit such as apples, pears, peaches or plums to buck it up.

METHOD

Pit the cherries and trim the other fruit, washing carefully if necessary. Heat the wine with the cassis and sugar in a saucepan, and bruise the stem of the basil and add. Bring to the boil and simmer for 5 minutes.

Remove the basil which will have imparted an aromatic, slightly clovey, flavour. Simmer each fruit for 30 seconds to a minute, depending on its ripeness, removing from the pan with a slotted spoon.

When all the fruit has been done whisk in the powdered gelatine, ensuring that it is not lumpy. Then replace all the fruit into the sugar syrup.

Line the sides of a cool 3 pint/1.5 litre bowl or pudding basin with the thinly sliced, de-crusted bread, then pour in the fruit mixture, covering the top with some more bread. Place a flat plate on the pudding and a light weight on top and chill in the refrigerator overnight.

When ready to serve, invert the bowl onto a serving dish so that the pudding will come from the mould. Decorate with a few extra fruits and serve with some lightly whipped fresh Jersey cream.

Serves 6-8.

GOOSEBERRY FOOL

INGREDIENTS
1lb/450g of gooseberries

A little water

4oz/110g of sugar

1/4 pint/150ml of double cream

2-3 heads of fresh elderflowers
if possible

CUSTARD
1/4 pint/150ml of milk

1/2 teaspoon/5ml of cornflower

2 egg yolks

A little sugar

OR USE
1/2 pint/275ml
of thick yoghurt

The flavour of elderflower greatly enhances gooseberry. You can now buy elderflower syrup, and so make this dessert all year round.

Many other fruits can be substituted for the gooseberries, eg raspberries, blackberries, plums, and damsons to make a variation on this theme. Nowadays I always use yoghurt instead of making custard!

METHOD

Wash the gooseberries, do not worry about the stems or stalks, cook them with a little water and sugar with the elderflower for 10-15 minutes until quite soft. Allow to cool then liquidise and sieve the mixture to form a fine purée.

To make the custard mix 1/4 pint/150ml of milk with 1/2 a teaspoon/2.5ml of cornflour and a little sugar and cook in a double saucepan over a gentle heat without boiling, stirring continually.

Take the two egg yolks and whisk with a little of the custard mixture, then pour this into the saucepan and mix thoroughly with a wooden spoon and cook for 5-10 minutes until the custard is smooth. Allow the mixture to cool.

Whip the cream well until firm. Stir in the yoghurt or custard and the gooseberry purée, and serve in a shallow glass bowl or a Paris goblet.

GREENGAGES
WITH FINO SHERRY

INGREDIENTS

1lb/450g of greengages

2oz/50g of sugar

¼ pint/150ml of water

*1 schooner/50ml
of Fino sherry*

*½ pint/275ml of lightly
whipped cream*

2 sprigs of lemon balm

These green plums have a fresh, sappy flavour. The clean, dry palomino fragrance mixes well with these which will now store in the refrigerator for weeks.

METHOD

Wash, halve and de-stone the greengages. Heat the water and sugar to make a light syrup. Add the greengages and cook, covered, for a minute.

Add the Fino sherry and cook for a further minute until just soft.

Snip the lemon balm leaves onto the greengages, and serve with the lightly whipped cream.

Prepared in this way they can be served hot or cold and are excellent in a fruit flan on a base of crème pâtisssière.

*OPPOSITE
GREENGAGES
WITH FINO SHERRY
garnished with lemon balm this
is a highly fragrant dessert*

PEAR FLAN WITH ALMONDS

INGREDIENTS

*4oz / 110g of sweet
shortcrust pastry*

2 pears, peeled and halved

¼ pint / 150ml of water

2oz / 50g of sugar

½ a lemon, de-juiced

1 passion fruit, de-pulped

*2oz / 50g of softened
unsalted butter*

2oz / 50g of ground almonds

1oz / 25g of caster sugar

½oz / 10g of flour

1 egg

The almond cream *Frangipani* is a good complement to many fruits prepared in this way. You may use cherries, peaches, nectarines, apples etc in a similar flan.

METHOD

Line a flan case with pastry. Make some sugar syrup with the water and sugar. Add the lemon juice and passion fruit (optional). Add the pear halves and poach gently for 3–5 minutes until just soft but still complete. Remove and cool. Reserve the liquid for a fruit salad or sorbet.

Work the butter soft in a bowl. Add the almonds and sugar slowly until a smooth paste is formed. Add the egg and flour and work well to form a smooth homogenous cream.

Spread this almond cream evenly on the pastry in the flan case to a maximum depth of ½"/1cm. Slice the half pears crossways thinly in ⅛"/3mm slices, cutting vertically through the flesh. Carefully flatten by pressing with the flat of the hand (like a pack of cards).

Using a pallet knife, lift in one at a time and place onto the almond cream, keeping each batch of slices intact, in a concentric pattern around the flan case.

Place in a pre-heated oven (mark 6/ 400°F/200°C) for about 30 minutes until the almond cream has risen and the whole flan is golden brown.

Serve hot or cold with cream or a fresh fruit, eg strawberries.

ELDERFLOWER FRITTERS

INGREDIENTS
4-8 heads of freshly picked
elderflowers – do not wash
these as the essential fragrances
will be rinsed away

BATTER
1 egg separated into
white and yolk

2oz/50g of plain flour

Pinch of salt

4oz/110g of fresh milk
or dry white wine

1 teaspoon/5ml
of caster sugar

Shallow or deep fat for frying

PURÉE
½lb/225g of gooseberries

The key to making a good fritter lies in the batter, and although many modern chefs have claimed to have invented the perfect batter, one only has to look in Mrs Beeton to find this recipe. Combined with the dusty-white flower of the elder bush, one has the most wonderful fritters.

METHOD

To make the batter, whisk the egg yolk with the flour, salt and milk (or wine), beat well, then leave to stand for 2 hours. When ready to prepare the dish, lightly whisk the egg white until it is thick and creamy but not forming stiff peaks, then fold the egg white into the batter, mix carefully to form a thick creamy lightly whipped cream consistency. Sweeten with a little granulated sugar.

Cut the fresh elderflowers from the thick stalks leaving a small thin stalk on each flower head, about 2"/5cm long. Then plunge into the batter so that a good amount holds up the flower head. Place into medium hot fat to quickly turn golden brown on either side. Remove and sprinkle with castor sugar and serve with the gooseberry and elderflower purée.

To make the gooseberry purée, simply cook ½lb/225g of gooseberries with 3-4 elderflower heads with a little water and sugar until all the fruit is tender. Allow to cool slightly, liquidise and press through a fine sieve and check the sweetness of the sauce. This is delicious served with the fritters and also with roast pork garnished with the elderflower fritters.

PEARS IN RED WINE & CINNAMON

INGREDIENTS

4 pears

Juice of one orange

4oz / 110g of sugar

½ bottle of full-bodied red wine,
eg Pinot Noir or Merlot

½ cinnamon stick

2 cloves

Pears are often under ripe and need to be 'brought on' by a short cooking. They present beautifully whether sliced or left whole.

METHOD

Combine the wine, sugar, orange juice and spices in a pan, bring to the boil and simmer for a few moments for the spices to infuse.

Peel the pears — you may either keep them whole or cut into slices lengthways. Add them to the pan and cook for about 15 minutes if left whole, 3–4 minutes if in slices. Take care they do not over-cook — the time will depend on the ripeness of the pears.

Check the juice for sweetness, adding a little extra sugar if necessary. Remove the pears and either serve hot or leave the juice to cool then pour over the pears and serve chilled with whipped cream or Greek yoghurt.

*OPPOSITE
PEARS IN RED WINE
& CINNAMON
pears in red wine lend
themselves well to a good
presentation*

MACERATED PEACHES IN LIQUEUR

INGREDIENTS

4 fresh peaches

¼ pint / 150ml of lemon and orange juice depending on how sharp you like the flavour

1 large measure / 50ml of orange aperitif, or vermouth bianco

2oz / 50g of caster sugar to taste

¼ pint / 150ml of lightly whipped cream or yoghurt

This uncooked dish uses the acidity of the citrus and herbiness of the vermouth to transform the flavour of the peaches.

METHOD

To skin the peaches either plunge into boiling water for 10-15 seconds, or lightly bruise the skin using the back of the knife scraping all over the peach. Then carefully remove the skin using the point of the knife.

Cut into segments and place in a bowl. De-juice the orange and lemons and grate a little of the zest into the juice.

Then add the sugar and aperitif, mixing well checking for sweetness. Pour over the peaches, stir them carefully and allow to macerate for 10-15 minutes minimum, or several hours if required. To serve, arrange the segments neatly in a concentric pattern on a shallow dish and serve with some light cream or yoghurt in the centre.

Kiwi Fruit with Toasted Peanuts

INGREDIENTS

8 kiwi fruits, peeled

*1 orange de-juiced
reserving some skin for the zest*

*2 teaspoons / 10ml
of clear honey*

2oz / 50g of unsalted peanuts

1oz / 25g of butter

Kiwi fruit – Chinese gooseberries – have been used as a garnish for almost every dish possible. I still like them and this dish uses them as the main ingredient. The sauce is enhanced and has a slightly crunchy topping.

METHOD

Toast the peanuts with a little butter taking care not to colour too darkly. Lightly crush by rolling under a bottle on a board and reserve.

Slice half the kiwis and arrange on four plates.

Using the softer ones for the sauce, press them through a fine sieve to remove most of the pips.

Stir in the honey and orange and grate a little zest into the sauce directly. You may add a little Cointreau or Grand Marnier. Mix well until smooth.

Spoon over the kiwi slices and top with toasted nuts. Some thick yoghurt is a good accompaniment.

INDEX TO RECIPES